Sabrina Ionescu: The Inspiring Story of One of Basketball's Star Guards

An Unauthorized Biography

By: Clayton Geoffreys

Copyright © 2024 by Calvintir Books, LLC

All rights reserved. Neither this book nor any portion thereof may be reproduced or used in any manner whatsoever without the express written permission. Published in the United States of America.

Disclaimer: The following book is for entertainment and informational purposes only. The information presented is without contract or any type of guarantee assurance. While every caution has been taken to provide accurate and current information, it is solely the reader's responsibility to check all information contained in this article before relying upon it. Neither the author nor publisher can be held accountable for any errors or omissions. Under no circumstances will any legal responsibility or blame be held against the author or publisher for any reparation, damages, or monetary loss due to the information presented, either directly or indirectly. This book is not intended as legal or medical advice. If any such specialized advice is needed, seek a qualified individual for help.

Trademarks are used without permission. Use of the trademark is not authorized by, associated with, or sponsored by the trademark owners. All trademarks and brands used within this book are used with no intent to infringe on the trademark owners and only used for clarifying purposes.

This book is not sponsored by or affiliated with the Women's National Basketball Association, its teams, the players, or anyone involved with them.

Visit my website at www.claytongeoffreys.com
Cover photo by NetsRepublic is licensed under CC BY-SA 4.0 / modified from original

Table of Contents

Foreword 1

Introduction 3

Chapter 1: Childhood and Early Life 10

Chapter 2: High School Career 18

Chapter 3: College Career 26

Chapter 4: WNBA Career 48

    Getting Drafted 48

    A Phantom Rookie Season 54

    A Second Rookie Season (Unofficially) 64

    An All-Star At 24 74

    One Step Closer to Championship Glory 81

Chapter 5: International Career 93

Chapter 6: Personal Life 100

Chapter 7: Impact and Legacy 104

Final Word/About the Author 115

References 121

Foreword

Sabrina Ionescu was drafted first overall by the New York Liberty in the 2020 WNBA Draft, marking the beginning of her professional basketball career. Before joining the Liberty, Ionescu played for the Oregon Ducks, where she established herself as a remarkable player. She was honored with the 2020 AP Player of the Year award and became the only NCAA player, regardless of gender, to achieve a career triple-double of 2,000 points, 1,000 assists, and 1,000 rebounds. With two WNBA All-Star selections and two All-WNBA Second Team awards to her name at the time of this writing, Ionescu continues to shine on the professional court. In 2023, she set a historic record in the WNBA 3-Point Contest by scoring 37 points, surpassing Stephen Curry's record of 31 points. Thank you for purchasing *Sabrina Ionescu: The Inspiring Story of One of Basketball's Star Guards*. In this unauthorized biography, we will learn Sabrina Ionescu's incredible life story and impact on the game of basketball. Hope you enjoy and if you do, please do not forget to leave a review!

Also, check out my website at claytongeoffreys.com to join my exclusive list where I let you know about my latest books. To thank you for your purchase, you can go to my site to download a free copy of *33 Life Lessons: Success Principles, Career Advice & Habits of Successful People*. In the book, you'll learn from some of the greatest thought leaders of different industries on what it takes to become successful and how to live a great life.

Cheers,

Clayton Geoffreys

Visit me at www.claytongeoffreys.com

Introduction

Over the course of the past decade or so, professional basketball has seen something of a statistical explosion. The pace of the game has sped up, emphasis on three-point shooting is at an all-time high, and teams are scoring significantly more points on average than they typically did in past eras.

Inevitably, these changes have also led to an abundance of personal statistics being collected by top players. Indeed, statistical output has become so robust among the best players in both the NBA and WNBA that it is common to hear that modern basketball is skewing the record books.

While the game itself may have evolved to allow for more impressive individual numbers, however, the bottom line is that there still need to be players capable of earning those numbers. Modern basketball *invites* statistical production, but there still have to be players who hone their talents and meet the challenge of that invitation. And few players in men's *or* women's basketball have been better suited to do this than Sabrina Ionescu.

One of the defining sensations of the century in college basketball and a budding star in the WNBA as well, Ionescu is a fit for the modern era, primarily because of her propensity to produce across statistical categories. She is unofficially recognized as the Queen of the Triple-Double, and there is perhaps no single statistical measure that better captures the evolving nature of modern basketball than the triple-double.

The triple-double is a term signifying that a player has collected double digits across three statistical categories in a single game. For instance, at least 10 points, 10 rebounds, and 10 assists. Once viewed as a somewhat rare achievement, it has become increasingly common at all levels of basketball. This, again, is thanks in part to the evolution of the game itself but has also been brought about by the extraordinary talents of a handful of leading players.

The shift first became apparent in the NBA, where triple-doubles have become significantly more common since the early 2010s. Before that, while triple-doubles were not unheard of, they were largely associated with just a few players throughout the history of professional basketball.

Oscar Robertson had been the first de facto king of these gaudy stat lines in the 1960s, and Wilt Chamberlain, famously a statistical wonder, earned his share of triple-doubles as well. Magic Johnson frequently recorded triple-doubles in the '80s and early '90s, and Grant Hill and Jason Kidd took up the mantle thereafter. Through the aughts and into the early 2010s, however, triple-double production increased. In 2016-17, it reached new heights when Russell Westbrook, then of the Oklahoma City Thunder, became the first player to *average* a triple-double over the course of an entire season, a feat only accomplished once previously when Oscar Robertson did so in 1961-62. Westbrook recorded the stat line 42 times that season. He then averaged a triple-double *again* in each of the next two seasons, and again in 2020-21!

Of course, Westbrook gathered the headlines and records, but he was not so much an outlier as the crest of a veritable triple-double wave. The year before Westbrook first averaged a triple-double, there had been just 75 of them total across the entire NBA. A decade before that, the number had been only 37. Last year, by contrast, there were 119 triple-doubles recorded across the NBA, and another player—the Denver Nuggets' Nikola Jokic—was 0.2 assists per game away from averaging a triple-double. He would have done so just six seasons after Westbrook, whereas the NBA waited 55 years to see Westbrook match the accomplishment of Robertson in 1961-62. This, more than anything else, illustrates the acceleration of the kind of comprehensive statistical production that

Sabrina Ionescu's game has proven to be so well suited to.

Interestingly, the phenomenon has not been unique to the NBA, either. With more minutes in each game and a lot more games being played, it is no surprise that the raw stats of NBA players still eclipse those of WNBA players. The rate at which wide-ranging statistical production is increasing, however, has also been evident in the WNBA.

Just recently, ESPN wrote an in-depth story examining the rise of the triple-double in women's professional basketball.[i] Per this story, there were only 11 total triple-doubles achieved over the WNBA's first 25 seasons of existence. Then, there were nine of them in the summer of 2022 alone.

If there is a single driver of the WNBA's growth in this area akin to Russell Westbrook in the NBA, it may be Alyssa Thomas. Sabrina Ionescu, however, was one of three players to record multiple triple-doubles amidst the 2022 explosion. And, notably, Ionescu accomplished this in just her third WNBA season, whereas Thomas was an established veteran in her ninth.

The same ESPN article that presented these numbers went to great lengths to shed light on the changes in professional basketball that have led to greater statistical output. For her part, however, Ionescu explained it in clear, simple terms. "As you're trying to evolve as a basketball player, you really want to be able to help in many categories aside from just one, because if Plan A doesn't work, you want to follow Plan B or C." This was a fascinating insight from this particular player because it described not only a strategic modern approach to basketball but, in fact, reflected upon Ionescu's own evolution as a player over time as well.

By her own account, a player with natural scoring ability, Ionescu could easily have honed her game with the objective of simply pouring in points. After all, it is the skill that comes most easily to her, and also the one that her basketball idol, the late Kobe Bryant, was best known for. However, instead of focusing only on producing points, Ionescu made a conscious decision to diversify her game from a young age. The result, all these years later, is a well-rounded talent who is at the forefront of women's basketball's triple-double movement. As such, Ionescu is positioned to become one of the defining stars of her era.

Chapter 1: Childhood and Early Life

Sabrina Ionescu was born in Walnut Creek, California, on December 6, 1997. Her parents, Dan Ionescu and Liliana Blaj, were Romanians who hailed from Bucharest. As was detailed in an article at *ESPN UK* in 2019, Dan and Liliana had made the choice to start a new life in America amidst the struggle of the Romanian Revolution in 1989.[ii] Part of a sequence of violent civil uprisings hailing the fall of the Soviet Union, this revolution ultimately led to the end of Communist rule in Romania. Before that outcome, however, the violence and uncertainty of the time led many families to seek greener pastures.

Dan Ionescu ventured to the United States first, joining relatives in northern California with the expectation of bringing his wife, Liliana, and their young son Andrei over soon thereafter. This proved more difficult than expected, though, and, in the end, the Ionescu family spent roughly five years apart.

"I was young," Dan Ionescu was quoted as saying in the aforementioned article. "I was looking at the future, and you just jump into the water. Trying to shoot for a better life, a better opportunity for the family ... not knowing what's on the other end. As time went by, it went harder. It was very hard. But what are your options? To fail or fight through."

Fighting through led to a happy outcome for the young Ionescu family, even if it took time to reach that point. By 1995, Liliana and Andrei were able to join Dan in northern California. At that point, Dan had also managed to turn a modest career as a taxicab driver into his own private limousine business. For all intents and purposes, he had captured the American dream for his family, leaving a war-torn region of Eastern Europe and establishing his own successful small business in California. This set the stage for the family to expand, and sure enough, by 1997, Liliana Blaj was pregnant—with twins.

Young Sabrina was born in December of that year, with her twin brother Eddy following 18 minutes later. As their mother described it, Sabrina assumed the role of older sister "by birthright and personality." By the time she was five years old, Sabrina was "ordering" *both* of her brothers to do their chores. At the same time, though, the siblings were close. The twins learned their parents' native language of Romanian together (as well as English), and would use it almost like a secret language, poking fun at people such that only the two of them could understand.

This language-based bond also came in handy when Sabrina and Eddy started to hit the basketball courts together; they could communicate in a way that their opponents could not, and thus gained advantages to "hustle" the competition.

Those trips to the basketball court started out of necessity, at least as Dan Ionescu recounted it. In the same *ESPN UK* article profiling the Ionescus' early days in the United States, Sabrina's father said, "I really didn't feel like having kids jumping on my head in the house. My incentive was, 'Can I just relax and watch some TV? How can I do that? So let's get them tired.'"

The process to "get them tired" was to drop the kids off at nearby Larkey Park, a 13-acre playground that was open all day and into the early evening. As the story goes, Sabrina and her brothers would play all day on some occasions, and Sabrina—despite the physical play, skinned knees and elbows, and being off on her own with boys—felt right at home.

"It wasn't like it is now where everyone is so ... I don't know," she reflected, alluding to the fact that a kid on a playground all day could feel safer back in the early 2000s. "I feel like there is more harm in the world now than there was back when we were younger."

Sabrina also recognizes that it was these long playground sessions, rather than the more conventional route of paid coaching or training, that set the tone for her basketball development.

"[My parents] were busy, they worked, so they dropped us off there, and we had each other, so that was easy. They never got me trainers. They just rolled the balls out and let me do whatever I wanted, and that's just what I took up."

Indeed, it could have been something other than basketball. There were tennis courts and other sporting options available in Larkey Park as well. But Sabrina and her brothers (and Eddy in particular) opted for basketball, and they regularly beat their opponents with a little help from covert communications in Romanian.

"Swear to God, we never lost," Eddy said years later as part of another family profile compiled by *The Oregonian*. He was referring back to those same playground games when he and Sabrina would play other duos with $5 on the line. They'd win, walk over to a nearby 7-Eleven convenience store, and buy Slurpees, as Sabrina fondly recalled.

Eventually, though, those happily-remembered childhood playground experiences gave way to increasingly more formal competition. Eddy joined youth teams, and when they were short a player, he would tell Sabrina to grab her sneakers. Just like that, she would be back on the court with the boys once more.

When Sabrina got to middle school, she was so much more comfortable with the boys (and with sports) that her parents got a call from a concerned guidance counselor. The counselor was worried that, without more female friends, Sabrina would have a difficult time socially.

Without enough girls to put together a basketball team, however, Sabrina would have a hard time making those female friends during her middle school days. Multiple sources have recalled the same counselor suggesting in a very literal way that Sabrina should take up playing with dolls. This was undoubtedly meant in a friendly and constructive manner, but it was also completely contrary to the very nature of Sabrina Ionescu. Sabrina was not about to change her ways or give up playing the game that she had already come to love. *Dolls, indeed!*

So, to that point, young Sabrina's response to the recommendation was to put together a team herself. Recalling this time in her life to a *Washington Post* reporter in 2019, Sabrina laughed at the "word-for-word" recommendation that she play with dolls.[iii] She then noted that, instead, she "went out and recruited a bunch of girls to sign up for the team." Effectively, she pieced together her own middle school girls' basketball team!

Soon thereafter, Sabrina Ionescu was on her way to Miramonte High School in Orinda, California. To say that she was already an emerging prospect might be a slight overstatement. It was true, however, that she had developed and honed a very natural passion for basketball. She had also "hardened" her abilities by playing on playgrounds and against boys, and had been committed enough to piece her own team together. At Miramonte, she would be better able to pursue her passion within an existing structure that could help her thrive.

Chapter 2: High School Career

Progressing from middle school to high school basketball is an adjustment for any young player. This is particularly true when the player is making the leap directly from eighth grade to the varsity ranks, as opposed to spending a freshman and/or sophomore year on a JV team. For Ionescu, though, the transition was eased by the fact that she was already familiar with the girls' head coach at Orinda's Miramonte High School.

In an *SEC Sports* article that came out the summer after Sabrina's freshman season, it was noted that said coach, Kelly Sopak, had helped guide the budding prospect through her travel basketball schedule since she had been in fourth grade.[iv] That mutual experience and familiarity lent Sabrina an element of comfort as she embarked on her high school career.

With that said, the same article noted that Sopak did not "just hand Ionescu a starting job" at the outset of her freshman year. Rather, he challenged her to earn the role by starting her just once every few games.

This was the arrangement until Sabrina seized the role with her undeniably fantastic play, and from that point on, there was no looking back. Over the course of her freshman season, she started 14 games and averaged 13.8 points, 3.9 assists, 6.1 rebounds, and 4 steals. This balanced and robust stat line was an early peek at the kind of comprehensive production Sabrina Ionescu would ultimately become known for.

"She played all five positions for us," Sopak reflected that summer after Sabrina's freshman year. "She is the type of player who, if she is playing a pickup game and notices her team doesn't have a center, she will play that spot." (This, despite the fact that Sopak had pegged Sabrina's weight at the time to be around 90 pounds!)

These comments were made in the midst of Ionescu's tryout for the U16 National Team, where Sue Phillips, the well-respected coach of a rival high school, would be in charge. Phillips, too, reflected positively on the nature of the sophomore-to-be's game. "She has put together a well-balanced game on both sides of the ball." She added that Sabrina was "just an asset when she's on the floor," and that she was an enthusiastic teammate as well.

These comments from Sopak and Phillips speak to how much of an impression Sabrina had made while leading Miramonte High School to a 27-3 record as a freshman. And, sure enough, as a sophomore, she got even better. With a year of experience under her belt, Sabrina demonstrated a notable improvement across all major statistical categories during the 2013-14 season. She finished the year averaging 18.7 points, 4.3 assists, 6.4 rebounds, and 4.3 steals per game. Miramonte High School went 30-2 that year and reached a high ranking of 23rd in the nation. The budding superstar from Walnut Creek had turned her school into a nationally relevant program.

Sabrina's junior year in high school in 2014-15 brought more of the same. Once again, she improved her production across every major statistical category. She averaged 23 points, 7.3 assists, 8.9 rebounds, 5 steals, and even an impressive 1 block per game. Miramonte High went 30-3, and this time reached a high ranking of 7th in the entire country.

On the local front, Sabrina led her teammates all the way to the semifinals of the California Interscholastic Federation (CIF) Open Division. This is a division in which the top schools compete for a title, regardless of size or regular season classification, thus making it, in some ways, the truest measure of California's best high school team in any given season.

Having fallen short in the CIF Open Division Semifinals, Sabrina attacked her senior season with a vengeance. Though she saw her rebounding and steal numbers drop slightly to 7.6 and 4.5 respectively, she had her best offensive performance yet, averaging 25.3

points and 8.8 assists over the course of the 2015-16 season.

Largely on the back of these sensational numbers, Miramonte High School made another deep run in the CIF Open Division Tournament, this time advancing all the way to the final. There, Sabrina pieced together one of the most impressive games of her high school career. She finished the first half with a buzzer-beating shot from halfcourt and wound up with 24 points, 10 assists, and 10 rebounds—yes, a *triple-double* in the Open Division championship! But, unfortunately, this wasn't quite enough to earn the win for her team; Miramonte fell to Chaminade, a perennial basketball powerhouse.

Sabrina finished her high school career without that elusive Open Division championship. In the effort to earn that title, however, she had established herself as one of the best women's basketball prospects in the United States. Furthermore, she had racked up the awards and honors to prove it. During and following her senior season, Sabrina was named Ms. Basketball in the state of California and won national Player of the Year recognition from *USA Today*, MaxPreps, and Gatorade. She was also invited to participate in the McDonald's All-American Game, an annual showcase featuring rosters of all-stars from across the nation.

At this game, Sabrina hit seven three-pointers to amass 25 points, throwing in 10 rebounds to earn MVP honors. She finished the season ranked by ESPN as the top point guard in the country and the #4 player in the Class of 2016.

Despite these impressive accomplishments, one major step had eluded Sabrina through the end of her senior season—she had yet to commit to a college program. It was known to some extent that she was intrigued by Oregon, although she also lent serious consideration to California and Washington. A *Washington Post* article noted that Ionescu also had opportunities to play at more established programs such as Oregon State and Texas.[iii]

In the end, it took Sabrina considerably longer than most top prospects in the country to make a decision, but she ultimately picked Oregon. She did so, as the same *Washington Post* article put it, because she wanted to "be *the* All-American at Oregon, not just *an* All-American somewhere else." Her desire to stand out rather than simply fit in may explain why Ionescu never appeared to give serious consideration to more traditional powerhouses like Connecticut or Tennessee.

Ionescu still did not make her commitment official until the summer of 2016, however, just before summer classes started for players at Oregon. When she and Oregon announced the commitment, though, Sabrina was very clear about her intention to stand out, and a connected desire to feel needed.

"I wanted to be the piece, not a piece in a program," she told *The Oregonian*.[v] "Both Oregon and Washington help me with that goal. At other schools, I was just 'a piece,' and they would be fine if I didn't go there, because they would have enough tools to still be able to win. Both of those schools make me feel like I'm really needed."

Despite her desire to be "the piece," Sabrina nevertheless arrived at Oregon that summer alongside several other highly touted basketball prospects. Head coach Kelly Graves described Sabrina and her fellow incoming Ducks as the class that could "define" the Oregon program.

So it was that Sabrina Ionescu headed off to college poised to chart her own path, bound for stardom with a program that had not traditionally attracted top talent.

Chapter 3: College Career

By spending much of the summer of 2016 on the University of Oregon campus in Eugene, Oregon, Sabrina Ionescu had given herself the opportunity to get comfortable with her college choice and teammates. She was part of what was meant to be a program-defining class of incoming freshmen, headlining the group alongside 6'4" forward Ruthy Hebard and 6'5" center Mallory McGwire.

At the same time, the Ducks and head coach Kelly Graves were coming off a reasonably strong season, having gone 24-11 overall and 9-9 in conference play in 2015-16. Ionescu and her fellow freshmen were not there to *save* the Ducks so much as to propel the rising program to new heights.

The season started with a win over Lamar on November 13th, with Ionescu contributing 11 points, 5 rebounds, and 3 assists. This was a rock-solid stat line for any freshman in her first game but it did not hint at the scoring ability or versatile production Ionescu was already known for.

However, it did not take long for her to make a bigger impression. Two games later, Ionescu scored 26 points in a win against UTSA, shooting 5-for-7 from three-point range in the process. Then, on November 27th, still in her first month of college competition, Ionescu led the Ducks in an away game at San Jose State, racking up 11 points, 12 rebounds, and 11 assists for her first NCAA triple-double. Less than three weeks later, she did it again, compiling 23 points, 12 rebounds, and 10 assists in a mid-December game all the way across the country at Clemson University.

With Sabrina having found an early groove, Oregon entered late December and the beginning of conference play in the Pac-12 with an impressive 10-2 record. During the 2016-17 season, however, the Pac-12 was a formidable gauntlet. The conference had four teams ranked in the preseason top 25 nationally; by the final week of December, there were five such teams, with three of them—Washington, UCLA, and Stanford—residing in the top 15.

As much promise as the young Oregon team had shown, the Ducks were not quite prepared for this level of competition. Accordingly, they went 8-10 in Pac-12 play, dropping their record on the season to 18-12 overall.

For her part, Ionescu continued to produce throughout the difficult conference slate, even managing two more triple-doubles. She had 14 points, 10 rebounds, and 13 assists in a win over Utah, and 11 points, 10 rebounds, and 10 assists when Oregon beat a UCLA team ranked 15th in the country at the time.

The Ducks fared somewhat better in the postseason. With Ionescu largely leading the way across major statistical categories, Oregon beat Arizona in the first round of the Pac-12 tournament before upsetting #11 Washington in a one-point game. The Ducks next lost to #10 Stanford but had done well enough to play their way off "the bubble" (a common term for the edge of NCAA Tournament consideration). Oregon was awarded the 10-seed in the NCAA Tournament's Bridgeport Regional. From this spot, the team made an unexpected and inspiring run.

In the opening rounds of the tournament commonly referred to as March Madness, Oregon sparked a little madness themselves, demonstrating grit and determination that belied their relative inexperience. The run started with an upset of 7-seed Temple, during which Ionescu delivered a trademark balanced performance, amassing 16 points, 7 rebounds, and 7 assists.

Sabrina was similarly effective in the next game, which saw the Ducks upset 2-seeded Duke, 74-65. Oregon next took on 3-seed Maryland and, having built up momentum with its first two wins, upset the

Terrapins behind 21 points, 6 rebounds, and 7 assists from Ionescu.

This win propelled Oregon to the final of the Bridgeport Regional and the so-called "Elite 8" of the NCAA Tournament. There, unfortunately, the team ran into top-seeded UConn, a perennial juggernaut. UConn triumphed with relative ease, but Oregon had made a strong statement by reaching the Elite 8 as a 10-seed, a feat even more impressive by the fact that they were led by a freshman. The prevailing sentiment was that they would be back before long.

As an individual, Sabrina Ionescu had pieced together a remarkable first season in Eugene. Accordingly, she was not only named the Pac-12 Freshman of the Year but was also voted unanimously onto the All-Pac-12 first team. Ionescu was also selected by the United States Basketball Writers Association as the National Freshman of the Year.

For Ionescu's sophomore year in 2017-18, Coach Graves was able to bring back most of the previous season's roster. He also added more talented young players in freshmen Satou Sabally and Anneli Maley. For the most part, though, the 2017-18 season was shaping up to be the Sabrina Ionescu Show. Sabrina had chosen Oregon in part to be "*the* piece," as she had made clear during her recruitment, and in her second year, that was just how she was positioned.

Ionescu shot out of the gates at full speed as a sophomore, notching two triple-doubles in Oregon's first three games: 29 points, 10 rebounds, and 11 assists in a win over Drake, and 16 points, 10 rebounds, and 11 assists when the Ducks traveled to Texas A&M to collect a road victory. Soon thereafter, Sabrina notched another triple-double with 21 points, 11 rebounds, and an impressive 14 assists as Oregon battled Ole Miss.

By the beginning of conference play in late December, Ionescu's brilliant and balanced play had led her team to an 11-2 record. Seemingly determined to set the tone for a better conference season this time around, Sabrina got off to such a hot start that she soon found herself setting a staggering record.

In just the second game of Pac-12 play for the Ducks, the multi-talented guard piled up 24 points, 14 rebounds, and 10 assists in a victory over Washington. This was her eighth collegiate triple-double, and in collecting it, Ionescu had already set the women's NCAA record for most such achievements in a career—in just December of her sophomore year!

"It's pretty surreal, to be honest," Ionescu reflected in a postgame recap.[vi] She kept her focus on her team, however, further noting that she was just happy they had won and gotten better. "As long as we continue to win, that's what's important to me. The triple-doubles just come."

For his part, Coach Graves praised Ionescu's consistent work ethic and intensity and said, "I'm honored to be her coach."

Ionescu's hot start to Pac-12 play had helped the Ducks get off to a smoother start. In fact, once the excitement of the triple-double record was behind Sabrina and her teammates, the team began to march through conference competition with a new confidence.

Oregon won its first six Pac-12 games, including contests against #14 UCLA and #18 Arizona State. They lost a rivalry game at #18 Oregon State, but then beat Oregon State two days later to start a fresh five-game winning streak. By the end of the regular season, the Ducks had put together a 16-2 conference record, winning the regular season title and earning the top seed in the conference tournament.

Oregon stayed hot in the conference tournament, dispatching Colorado by nearly 40 points in the opening round before toppling a UCLA team that was ranked #9 in the country at the time. This took the Ducks to the Pac-12 Final, where they clobbered #16 Stanford, 77-57. It was a somewhat lopsided affair, though much of the difference came down to Sabrina Ionescu. Even though her 4 rebounds and 4 assists in the final were slightly below her lofty standards, the 36 points she scored represented a career high at that point. She shot 10-for-14 from the field and 4-for-10 from three to take command of the game and ensure a Pac-12 Tournament championship for Oregon.

The team's exceptional regular season and Pac-12 Tournament performances earned it the 2-seed in the NCAA Tournament's Spokane Regional. And, once again, the Ducks went on a little bit of a run, albeit from a position of strength this time.

Oregon trounced Seattle and Minnesota in the first two rounds by 43 and 28 points, respectively. Then, the team got a bit of a lucky break facing 11-seed Central

Michigan in the Sweet 16 but took care of business with an 83-68 victory. Ionescu had 16 points, 9 rebounds, and 10 assists, missing a triple-double by just one rebound. So, just like that, Oregon was back in the Elite 8 for a second straight season. Once again, however, the team ran into an extremely difficult opponent in 1-seed Notre Dame. The Fighting Irish overcame a 26-point effort from Ionescu to win 84-74, advancing to the Final Four and eventually winning the whole tournament.

Once again, despite the season ending with a hard loss, the perception was that Oregon had made significant progress and would be a very real threat moving forward. And, once again, Sabrina Ionescu wrapped up the season with a collection of individual awards. She was again selected to the All-Pac-12 first team, and this time earned Pac-12 Player of the Year honors as well. Nationally, Ionescu was named a first team All-American by ESPN and became a finalist for the Naismith Award, which recognizes college basketball's best player. She also won the Nancy Lieberman Award, given to the country's best point guard each year.

The 2018-19 season marked Sabrina Ionescu's junior year, and once again Oregon had the benefit of continuity. Save for guard Lexi Bando, who had graduated the previous spring, the Ducks returned all of their key contributors. It was thus unsurprising that they got off to another hot start in non-conference play, rolling to an 11-1 record through late December.

Toward the end of this early slate of competition, Sabrina Ionescu once again made history. The Ducks squared off against Air Force on December 20th in what might have been an unremarkable game. Oregon won 82-36. In the midst of this lopsided victory, however, Ionescu had notched another triple-double, finishing with 17 points, 11 rebounds, and 13 assists. It was her third triple-double of the year, but her 13th overall. That meant that it broke her tie with one-time

BYU star Kyle Collinsworth. And, while Ionescu already had the NCAA women's record, Collinsworth had previously held the overall *men's* NCAA record with 12 triple-doubles.

Almost dismissively, Ionescu said of her latest accomplishment, "Yeah, I guess, awesome. Just another day."[vii] She then clarified that there had been some pressure from others anticipating the milestone and that it would be a relief not "hearing it all the time" from people around her. "I'm happy it's behind me now and I can just focus on what I can do in order for us to win."

True to the notion of moving on and helping her team win, Ionescu managed another triple-double in her very next game, her 13 points, 10 rebounds, and 14 assists helping Oregon to triumph over UC-Irvine. This helped set the tone for a Pac-12 slate during which the reigning Player of the Year would continue to have extraordinary individual efforts in the conference and the Ducks would continue to win.

Throughout the conference season, Ionescu piled up three more triple-doubles; she also broke the Oregon program's record for assists in a career when she collected her 609th in a win at USC. Along the way, Oregon hardly stumbled, ultimately finishing with a 16-2 record in conference play. This was enough for another regular season title and allowed them to secure the top seed in the Pac-12 Tournament for the second year running, and a #6 national ranking heading into the postseason.

In the Pac-12 Tournament, Oregon beat Arizona 77-63 and then prevailed in a thrilling overtime game against #25 UCLA. They next faced #7 Stanford in the Pac-12 Final and came up just short, losing 64-57 despite a 27-point, 12-rebound effort from Ionescu.

Oregon entered March Madness as the #2 seed in the Portland Regional. The team eased into action with an easy 78-40 victory over Portland in the opening round. The Ducks then faced a slightly trickier 10-seed in Indiana but won by 23 points thanks to a monstrous game from Ionescu. The star guard finished with 29 points, 10 rebounds, and 12 assists, marking her best NCAA Tournament performance to date.

The Ducks next faced 6-seed South Dakota State in the Sweet 16 and won to advance to a third straight Elite 8. There, they finally got over the hump, upsetting 1-seed Mississippi State 88-84 behind 31 points, 7 rebounds, and 8 assists from Ionescu. The junior sensation had led her team all the way to the Final Four, though that was as far as their run would go. Oregon played a tight game against eventual champion Baylor but lost in the end, 72-67.

At the end of the season, Ionescu was once again showered with awards. She was first team All-Pac-12 and made the AP All-American team for the second time. For the second year in a row, she won both the

Nancy Lieberman Award and Pac-12 Player of the Year. And this time around, she also won the Wade Trophy and John Wooden Award, two of a handful of different awards that are designed to recognize college basketball's top player.

Following the loss in the 2019 Final Four, Sabrina Ionescu's college career hung in the balance. By age, she was now eligible for the WNBA draft; academically, she was already poised to graduate from Oregon. There was no necessity to return to school for a senior season, and, in fact, many people believed that she would make the decision to go pro. In the end, however, she decided to return to Eugene one more time, not to graduate or even necessarily prepare herself for professional basketball, but to finish what she had started.

Writing her own address to the Oregon faithful through *The Players' Tribune*, Sabrina started with a story about finding out that NBA legend Kobe Bryant had done a video with ESPN breaking down her game.[viii] She used this to express that many seemed to think she'd already accomplished every possible dream, and that she'd had it as good as it gets. But, she clarified, "This is NOT as good as it gets."

Ionescu argued that people suggesting she had it all did not understand the mission she and her teammates had been on. She walked back through her progress with the program, losing badly in the Elite 8 as a freshman, nearly winning an Elite 8 matchup as a sophomore, and finally, reaching the Final Four as a junior. Without making explicit predictions, she emphasized that she and her teammates had unfinished business, and that they were *building* something in Eugene. "We're building a program that wins national championships," she wrote. "Starting, I hope, with this next one."

It was a thoughtful and inspiring return announcement that made it crystal clear that Ionescu and her teammates expected to be the team to beat during the 2019-20 season. Once again, they had continuity on their side, not just because Ionescu was coming back but also because she was being joined by the remaining core of Satou Sabally, Ruthy Hebard, and Erin Boley. The Ducks were ranked #1 in the country in preseason polls.

The non-conference season went nearly perfectly for Oregon. The team went 10-1, with their lone loss coming against #8 Louisville. They entered the Pac-12 season looking every bit the contenders they were expected to be during the preseason. From that point forward, Sabrina Ionescu went on something of a rampage, producing one spectacular performance after another and racking up fresh records along the way.

In an 87-55 romp over #3 Stanford, Ionescu had exploded for a career-high 37 points to go along with 11 rebounds and 7 assists. The performance had helped the Ducks overcome a slow first quarter and also established Ionescu as Oregon's all-time leading scorer.

"She seems to always do it on nights like this, too," Coach Kelly Graves said, alluding to Ionescu's propensity for breaking out her best performances against elite opponents or with a lot on the line.[ix]

Continuing this trend soon thereafter, Ionescu had another record-breaking performance in a win over rivals Oregon State, then ranked #7 in the country. This time, she seized the all-time record for most assists in the Pac-12—by men or women. The record had previously been held by NBA great Gary Payton, who personally reached out to congratulate her on the spectacular achievement.

In late February, Sabrina faced a unique challenge. Between this time and discovering that Kobe Bryant had made a video breaking down her game for ESPN and this point, she had actually established a relationship with the LA Lakers legend. Bryant had effectively mentored her, and she, in turn, had grown close with his family. So, it came to be that, when Bryant and one of his young daughters tragically passed away in a helicopter accident, Ionescu was asked to speak at the memorial service. She did just that, traveling to the Staples Center in LA and speaking powerfully to a crowd of family, friends, and former teammates. It was a visibly emotional experience for Sabrina, yet her teammates needed her as well.

From the Staples Center, she traveled straight to Stanford, where Oregon was to play a #4-ranked Cardinal team that evening. The Ducks won 74-66 behind 21 points, 12 rebounds, and 12 assists from Ionescu. It was her eighth triple-double of the season, and it led her to become the first player in NCAA history to record 2,000 points, 1,000 rebounds, and 1,000 assists in a career.

Ionescu and her Ducks were flying high, and Oregon entered the Pac-12 Tournament a couple of weeks later with a stalwart 17-1 conference mark. They were the top seed and were ranked #3 nationally. Ionescu and her teammates were dominant in an opening win over Utah, and then beat #13 Arizona by 18 points. That took them into the Pac-12 Final and another rematch with Stanford. Ionescu had 20 points, 8 rebounds, and 12 assists to lead the Ducks to an emphatic 89-56 win. With that Pac-12 Tournament win, Oregon solidified their #2 ranking in the country. As expected, the team was in the thick of contention for an NCAA title.

Unfortunately, four days after the win over Stanford, the 2020 NCAA Tournament was canceled. It was at this time that the deadly COVID-19 virus was first beginning to spread across the United States and fears of a pandemic were taking hold. Furthermore, there were no vaccines yet, and there was no way of ensuring player or fan safety.

As such, it turned out that the Pac-12 championship had been Sabrina Ionescu's final college game. Though the Ducks were well positioned to compete for a national championship, their pursuit was cut short by circumstances beyond anyone's control.

After the season, Sabrina Ionescu won just about every award conceivable. She was first team All-Pac-12 and All-American; she won Pac-12 Player of the Year and the Nancy Lieberman Award each for the third time; she won both the Wade Trophy and the John Wooden Award for the second year running. This time, Ionescu also captured national Player of the Year honors from the USBWA and AP and was awarded the Honda Sports Award and the Naismith Award, both of which recognize the best collegiate player of the year.

Though it was a shame that Sabrina Ionescu and her teammates did not get to contend for their championship, just about everything else had gone right. Ionescu was the undisputed best player in college basketball, and she had proven that she could lead a true contender. Moreover, she had put a capstone on one of the greatest NCAA basketball careers in history.

Now, a year after many had expected her to make the pro leap, she was ready to progress to the WNBA.

Chapter 4: WNBA Career

Getting Drafted

As Sabrina Ionescu finally turned her attention toward her professional career, the circumstances surrounding the impending WNBA draft became strange. Early spread of the COVID-19 virus in the U.S. had necessitated that the draft move to a virtual format, rather than the typical in-person ceremony. Furthermore, there was uncertainty about how the coming season would play out. Usually, the WNBA season follows the draft quite closely, however, in the spring of 2020, it was not entirely clear that the season could be played at all.

But while the season to come was shrouded in uncertainty, Sabrina Ionescu's fate in the draft was anything but. Strange circumstances did not affect teams' priorities, and there was near-universal agreement that the New York Liberty, slated to pick first, would select the University of Oregon superstar.

Sports and pop culture site The Ringer, in its WNBA mock draft, eschewed predictions in favor of certainty, stating simply that "the best NCAA D-1 player—male or female—in history will go No. 1."[x] The write-up described Ionescu as having set a new standard for the sport and defined her skillset as "everything" and the Liberty's selection as a "no-brainer."

Writers at The Athletic, meanwhile, were similarly effusive in assessing Ionescu's draft prospects.[xi] One called the Liberty's selection "the easiest pick of the entire draft and a chance to usher in a new era" for the franchise, noting that Ionescu was a "generational player" who could attract new fans in addition to producing on the court. Another spoke more to the Oregon star's game, calling her "easily one of—if not the most—complete players" in the draft and highlighting her "unmatched" floor vision and statistical output. This writer also pointed out that Ionescu's drive and competitiveness were essentially invaluable, and that, at Oregon, these attributes had turned sparse crowds into sellouts over the course of four years in Eugene.

Even the title of the mock draft at The Athletic spoke to the confidence that the basketball world had in Ionescu's selection at the top: "The Athletic's 2020 WNBA Mock Draft: How Will It Unfold After No.1?" The No. 1 pick, this title implied, was a foregone conclusion.

Additional mock drafts at outlets such as ESPN, CBS Sports, and the WNBA news and commentary platform Swish Appeal all agreed. By returning to college for a record-breaking senior season, Ionescu had established herself as the best professional prospect in basketball. By changing the nature of Oregon's program and raising the very profile of women's college basketball, she had also proven that she could have an impact beyond the court. Ionescu was the epitome of a surefire No. 1 pick.

That pick, as mentioned, would belong to the New York Liberty. The once-proud franchise was coming off back-to-back dismal seasons during which it went 7-27 and 10-24, respectively. As such, it was undergoing a significant overhaul that went well beyond the WNBA draft.

For starters, head coach Katie Smith had been let go at the end of her contract, paving the way for Walt Hopkins, a Minnesota Lynx assistant coach, to take over. The Liberty were also under new ownership, having been sold to Joe Tsai and Clara Wu Tsai, the owners of the NBA's Brooklyn Nets. Thus, the team was preparing to move to Barclays Center in Brooklyn to play its home games in the same arena that the Nets use and was even transitioning to a new logo and overall aesthetic.

Plus, changes on the court were being set in motion as well. In a pre-draft blockbuster deal, the Liberty traded longtime star and all-time franchise scoring leader

Tina Charles to the Washington Mystics in a three-team deal that boosted New York's depth and draft equity.

In short, the Liberty were a franchise in need of a significant overhaul, and they were meeting that need in aggressive fashion. A shuffled roster, a new arena, a new owner, and even new logos and uniforms made for a sense that this was almost a wholly new team taking the place of the version of the Liberty that had been part of the WNBA since its inception in 1997.

Of course, this overall feeling of newness made the opportunity to select Sabrina Ionescu seem all the more perfect. It was as if a new franchise had sprouted in Brooklyn just in time to pick up a player who could double as a franchise star on the court and be a main attraction to fans as well.

When the virtual WNBA draft finally came along, there was no suspense surrounding the top pick. The Liberty selected Sabrina Ionescu. Right away, there was a sense that it was a big moment, not only for New York but also for the entire WNBA. To that point, a *New York Times* recap of the draft quoted league commissioner Cathy Engelbert as saying, "A big priority of mine is to focus on marketing the league and our players. Driving household names and engaging them with fans in a different way is a thing we're continuing to work on."[xii]

The comment was somewhat indirect, but it was a clear allusion to Ionescu's potential not only as a player but also as an *attraction* for the WNBA. She was someone who could produce stats and wins on the court and drive engagement off of it.

For her part, Sabrina reacted to her number-one selection with a sense of relief, hanging her head before burying it in her hands. Per the same *New York Times* recap, she was asked what had gone through her mind and responded, "That I'm blessed. I've been working for this for my entire career and just super excited to be able to see that come to fruition." She also commented on the Liberty's strong guard play, indicating that she had done her homework and was excited to join her new teammates.

All at once, Sabrina Ionescu had transitioned from a college legend to the face of the franchise for a New York Liberty team that was embarking on a new chapter. Before touching her first WNBA ball, she already had an endorsement deal with Nike and was being billed, more or less, as the future of the league (or at least a big part of it). Now, all that was left was to find out if and when her rookie season would start, as the budding COVID-19 pandemic hung ominously over the sports world and had already claimed numerous lives.

A Phantom Rookie Season

As WNBA officials debated how to handle the rising pandemic as safely as possible, the WNBA season failed to start on time. Rather than canceling the season entirely, however, the league ultimately decided to do something similar to what the NBA had done to finish its 2019-20 season and playoffs. Specifically, they elected to play a shortened season of just 22 games, with all of the action set to take place in a "bubble" environment at the IMG Academy in Bradenton, Florida.

The "bubble" would effectively be a quarantine zone, such that everyone who needed to be present for the season to take place would be on the inside, and there would be very little coming and going. This way, players and league officials could be reasonably confident that the season could be played without high risk of a COVID-19 outbreak.

What ultimately came about in Florida was very much an incomplete season. Several prominent players elected to skip what had affectionately been dubbed the "Wubble" (for WNBA bubble) because of health concerns. The likes of Liz Cambage, Tina Charles,

Natasha Cloud, and even 2019 WNBA MVP Elena Delle Donne were granted medical waivers to miss the season. Additionally, the 22-game slate essentially represented just two-thirds of a typical 34-game season.

At the same time, there was a great deal of admiration for the WNBA for their diligence with which they prepared the Wubble. Player health and safety had been prioritized accordingly, and a makeshift season had been pieced together on the fly amidst immensely difficult circumstances.

The new-look Liberty entered the Wubble as an exceedingly young team. First-time head coach Walt Hopkins was leading a roster that featured 7 rookies among 12 total players. The team figured to be led by a pair of UConn products in Kia Nurse and Kiah Stokes, who had six years of combined experience in the league. That is, until Ionescu took the reins, which most people had expected to see happen early in her career.

The Wubble season officially got underway on July 25, 2020, and Sabrina Ionescu—one of the greatest college players in history and a strong candidate for the next face of the WNBA—took the court for the first time in an isolated environment that was without fans.

Sabrina struggled in her first outing, shooting just 4-for-17 from the field for 12 points, although she did manage to add 6 rebounds and 4 assists, flashing some of her trademark well-roundedness. The revamped young Liberty squad lost by 16 points to a talented Seattle Storm team led by Breanna Stewart and Sue Bird. This made for an interesting matchup, given that Stewart was another young star of the sort Ionescu seemed destined to become and Bird, a veteran point guard, was one of the few players to whom Ionescu's game could somewhat reasonably be compared.

While Ionescu had a difficult opening game against Seattle and its stars, there was no prolonged struggle to kick off her rookie campaign. In just her second game, this time against the Dallas Wings, the first-year guard took charge of proceedings as if she were back on her home court at the University of Oregon.

Shooting 11-for-20 from the field and a sizzling 6-for-10 from three-point range, Ionescu led all scorers with 33 points. She also racked up seven rebounds and seven assists, providing the sense that it was just a matter of time before she would be back to her triple-double ways at the professional level. The Liberty ultimately lost that game by 13 points, however, with Ionescu's former college teammate, Satou Sabally, being among the standouts for Dallas. Despite the loss, Ionescu had made a powerful statement. In just her second game, she had looked every bit the part of a WNBA superstar.

Unfortunately, the excitement generated by this outstanding second-game performance would prove to be short-lived. The Liberty next took to the Wubble hardwood on July 31st against the Atlanta Dream, and Ionescu once again got off to a hot start. She shot 4-for-5 to rack up 10 points in the first 12 minutes of the contest. At that point, however, Ionescu stepped down on opponent Betnijah Laney's foot in the middle of game action, turning her ankle in the process and ultimately needing to be helped off the court. She missed the remainder of the game as the Liberty fell to 0-3 on the season.

Ionescu was taken to an area hospital and diagnosed with a grade-3 ankle sprain. This is effectively the most severe form of sprain. It means that the ankle ligament has been completely ruptured, and the recovery time can be several months. During the initial assessment and at a follow-up with specialists in New York, though, it was determined that Ionescu did not need to have surgery to repair her ligament. She simply needed to rest and recover, and, in doing so, she would miss the remainder of the abbreviated 2020 season. Thus, Sabrina's rookie campaign had come to a close after just two-and-a-half games, and without her, the depleted Liberty sputtered to a 2-20 record in the Wubble.

This was, without a doubt, a disappointing way for a budding superstar's rookie season to go. What was telling, however, was the way in which the basketball community responded to Ionescu's misfortune.

The injury itself inspired reporting efforts by the likes of Ramona Shelburne and Shams Charania, dedicated insiders who normally cover the NBA rather than the WNBA; Ionescu's brand was already so big that both reporters took time away from their typical beats to update the public on her injury.

Ionescu also received public support from none other than LeBron James, who expressed his dismay at the injury and wished her swift healing on Twitter.

Perhaps most interesting of all, though, was the basketball royalty with whom Ionescu chose to spend some of her time while rehabbing. Separated from basketball due to her ankle and unable to do much rehab in a team setting because of the pandemic, Ionescu visited Kobe Bryant's family. Sabrina appeared to draw comfort from being among the wife and daughters of her late mentor, having remained close with the family since Kobe's passing.

In an interview with NBA reporter Marc Stein at the *New York Times*, Ionescu was asked if it had been helpful for her to spend time with the Bryants and grieve collectively.[xiii] "I think it's helped all of us, just to be able to see each other, be around each other, tell stories, obviously be there for the good and the bad times, whatever it is," she responded. "I'll always be close to his family, and I think they know that they'll always be close to me. So it's been great to be able to just spend time with them, and that's honestly been a blessing that I've been able to have that opportunity to be down in L.A. and see them."

While Ionescu did not draw a direct line between her time with the Bryants and her mindset regarding her injury, it is not hard to imagine that the perspective she gained from Kobe's passing helped her stay measured about her own bad luck. When Stein asked her in the same interview how she dealt with the shock of a serious injury so early in her career, she responded, "It happens. It really wasn't the end of the world … I just kind of took it for what it was and moved on." Spoken like someone who knew already, at a young age, that there were worse things in life than a sprained ankle.

Ionescu was similarly measured about the state of her rehab. Asked by Stein how much she was able to do at that time, nearly two months after the injury, she answered, "I'm able to do just about everything that I want. I'm not playing live now and probably won't be for a while, just because there's no point playing live.

It's not necessarily for my health or my ankle, but just due to COVID-19 and everything going on." Regarding her competitive drive and eagerness to get back to WNBA action, she added, "I'm actually pretty patient. I'm just making sure I'm staying healthy. There's nothing really I'm rushing back for, so I think that's definitely helped me ... I have a while until next season, so I think this is going to be a time to just get my body where I want it to be." She did, however, express that she was excited to get to New York, rather than the Wubble, and play in front of fans at Barclays Center in 2021.

Not long after her in-depth interview with Marc Stein and what seemed to be positive updates on her health, Ionescu did end up undergoing a minor surgery on her injured ankle. Rather than addressing ligament damage, however, her procedure was to remove a small piece of bone that had become loose during the injury and had since become irritating. The surgery was successful, and Ionescu's ligament was subsequently declared to be fully healed. So, while there was a slight setback, she remained on track to ramp up her basketball activity and prepare to return to the Liberty for the 2021 season.

A Second Rookie Season (Unofficially)

For the 2021 season, the WNBA opted for a return to normal. The Wubble had been a success under the circumstances, but a year later the league was getting back to a version of an ordinary format. The season was to be very slightly abbreviated, and schedules were adjusted to minimize travel. For all intents and purposes though, the 2021 season was to be a normal one.

Fully recovered from her ankle injury, Sabrina Ionescu approached this season as a sort of second rookie year. In fact, a preseason article at *Insider* revealed that the Liberty star-in-waiting even suggested the WNBA should designate her officially as a rookie.[xiv] But, as far as that idea went, the league had other plans. "I don't think that they allowed me to be classified as a rookie again because I played two games," Ionescu said on the subject. "But I am referring to myself as this being my first year, because I played two games."

She further expressed that she felt she had missed out on the traditional rookie experience by not being able to play against most of the other teams in the league and by having no chance to compete for a Rookie of the Year award (which she would likely have won). She added that it did not really "make a lot of sense" for the league to consider 2021 her second season.

Nonetheless, Ionescu also made it clear that she was eager to get back on the court in an official capacity. "I've been awaiting this time for a while now after being hurt last season," she told *Insider*. "So I'm really excited to just start playing, for games to start, and fans to be in the arena."

It was clear that whatever the league's official designation of her status, Ionescu herself was approaching 2021 as a fresh start. And the New York Liberty were doing the same. In fact, while Ionescu had been rehabilitating her ankle and working her way back into basketball activities in the early months of 2021, the New York front office had been busily reshaping its roster. There was a clear need for improvement following a dismal two-win season, and while Ionescu's return would offer a boost, it was clear that she would need some help even when performing at her best.

Somewhat ironically, the Liberty's first major move was to sign free agent Betnijah Laney, a sixth-year guard/forward out of Rutgers—and the very player upon whose foot Sabrina Ionescu had twisted her ankle. The contact had been purely accidental, of course, but it seemed an odd twist of fate that Laney would now be Ionescu's teammate. That said, Laney had averaged 17.2 points, 4.9 rebounds, and 4 assists for Atlanta during the previous season and thus represented a significant upgrade for New York.

Meanwhile, the Liberty also traded Kia Nurse for future pick equity and traded some of their own stashed picks as well for 6'2" forward Natasha Howard, who was fresh off a WNBA Championship with the Seattle Storm in the Wubble. And in another transaction with the Storm, New York traded the rights to Stephanie Talbot for 5'10" guard Sami Whitcomb. Finally, the team also drafted a 6' forward named Michaela Onyenwere out of UCLA.

Together, these four new acquisitions—Laney, Howard, Whitcomb, and Onyenwere—would make up the core of the 2021 Liberty alongside Ionescu. The team had entirely changed its composition.

Armed with this revamped and refreshed roster, the Liberty shot out of the gate, winning its first two games of the season, both of which were against the Indiana Fever. Incidentally, these games both counted toward the inaugural Commissioner's Cup as well. This was an entirely new in-season competition that had originally been scheduled to launch in 2020 but had been pushed back a year due to the COVID-shortened season. This added a little more excitement to the Liberty's 2-0 start, but it was the quality of play that was most encouraging of all. Sabrina Ionescu made a strong statement in the first of the two games, showcasing her full health with 25 points and 11 assists in front of the New York fans at Barclays Center.

Following their 2-0 start, Ionescu finally had the sort of breakout fans had expected from the moment she'd been drafted. The Liberty hosted the Minnesota Lynx in what was still only Ionescu's fifth full game as a professional player. The former number-one pick erupted for 26 points, 10 rebounds, and 12 assists, shooting 4-for-7 from three-point range en route to her first triple-double in the WNBA.

It was the first such accomplishment in the history of the Liberty franchise, and just the 10th the WNBA had ever seen. At 23, Ionescu also became the *youngest* WNBA player to post a triple-double. It was a remarkable announcement that the Sabrina Ionescu everyone had watched at the University of Oregon could, in fact, dominate in a similar manner at the professional level. Given Ionescu's history of shrugging off personal achievements to focus on team success, however, it is likely that Sabrina was more pleased by the fact that New York won the game to improve to 3-0 on the season.

Ionescu did not stay quite as hot in her next few outings, but she was still beginning to make a habit of well-rounded production, just the way she had in college. She collected 10 points, 6 rebounds, and 5 assists as New York suffered its first loss of the season against the Mystics in Washington. She then notched 19 points, 5 rebounds, and 12 assists in a win at Chicago. These performances were enough to earn Ionescu the honor of Eastern Conference Player of the Week, a remarkable achievement, given how little

WNBA experience she actually had under her belt at that point. Meanwhile, the Liberty had improved to 4-1 (and 3-1 in games counting toward Commissioner's Cup competition).

Ionescu played well in the next game as well when New York beat Dallas to move to a surprising 5-1 on the season. Thereafter, however, her performance began to tail off a bit, along with the Liberty's winning ways.

Ionescu failed to break the double-digit scoring barrier in her next seven outings. The Liberty went 1-6 across those seven games. At first, this appeared to be a somewhat random and unexpected slump for the typically relentless Ionescu. But, in time, it became apparent that she was not playing at full health. In fact, it came to light that she was dealing with tendinitis in the same ankle that she had injured during the previous season.

"I think putting a ton of load on that leg/foot/ankle/shin after, you know, a long recovery process, I think it just was a lot for her body to handle," Liberty coach Walt Hopkins was quoted in a 247Sports piece.[xv] "We just need to get her a little rest and hopefully she'll be back real soon."

Ionescu sat out for the Liberty's win over the Phoenix Mercury and was listed as day-to-day while she dealt with the tendinitis. She did not stop playing entirely, but for the next few weeks of the season, she was in and out of the lineup, playing fewer minutes and accordingly producing less. It was perhaps a stroke of luck, however, that less than a month after Ionescu sat out the Phoenix game, the WNBA took an unusual hiatus. This was so that players from around the league could travel to Tokyo to take part in the Summer Olympics, which had been delayed from the previous summer.

For Sabrina, this break was a chance to get some much-needed rest for her leg in the hope that she could return to full health when the league resumed play in mid-August.

When the Liberty returned to action on August 15th, they were 10-11. Up to that point, Ionescu had averaged 9.9 points, 5.7 rebounds, and 6 assists on the season. These would be excellent numbers for almost any second-year player, but everyone who had seen Ionescu at full strength knew that she could be doing better. The good news was, when she suited up for the resumption of the season, she was back to full strength, or at least close to it. The bad news was, by that point, the Liberty's season appeared to be unrecoverable.

Indeed, even with Ionescu back on board, New York finished the season with a dismal 2-9 stretch, finishing 12-20 overall in the abbreviated 32-game season. However, if there was a bright spot during this final stretch of the season, it was that Sabrina Ionescu began to establish a rhythm for the first time since the first week of the season. She most notably upped her scoring production down the stretch, averaging 14.8 points, 5.6 rebounds, and 6.3 assists in those last 11 games.

Despite the poor finish to the season, the Liberty still found themselves in an opening-round playoff game against the Mercury. It was a single-elimination game, and one in which New York nearly shocked the WNBA with an upset. Ionescu had a strong playoff debut, finishing with 14 points, 5 rebounds, and 11 assists. In the end, though, the Liberty fell by just one point, 83-82.

For the season, Sabrina Ionescu finished with averages of 11.7 points, 5.7 rebounds, and 6.1 assists per game, shooting 44.7% from the field and 32.5% from three. She was not up to her own towering standards just yet, but overall, she had started to show hints of rounding into form. It is also worth noting that if the WNBA *had* allowed Ionescu to be labeled a rookie in 2021, she would undoubtedly have won the Rookie of the Year vote in a landslide.

But, as it was, the award actually went to her teammate, Michaela Onyenwere. The UCLA product had finished her debut season with the Liberty with averages of 8.6 points, 2.9 rebounds, and 0.6 assists. These numbers represented a strong rookie campaign, but clearly it was nothing like what Ionescu had done in what was effectively her first full season as a professional.

An All-Star At 24

After a 12-20 finish and a single-game postseason experience, the Liberty once again set about making offseason changes that would impact the trajectory of Sabrina Ionescu's career. This time, the main change was on the bench. New York decided to let Walt Hopkins go and welcomed Sandy Brondello as the team's new head coach. A WNBA All-Star herself back in 1999, Brondello was already an experienced coach. She won the WNBA title with the Phoenix Mercury in 2014 and had remained with that team through the 2021 season. Now, the hope was that her practiced hand could help lead a talented young Liberty team toward playoff contention.

As for personnel, the Liberty made two significant free-agent signings, bringing in 6'5" center Stefanie Dolson and 5'10" guard Marine Johannes. These two would end up comprising the Liberty's 2022 core alongside Natasha Howard, Betnijah Laney, and Ionescu. The team also had another high draft selection, using their 5th pick on rising Oregon star (and Sabrina's former Duck teammate) Nyara Sabally. However, the rookie wound up needing to undergo a major medical procedure that caused her to miss the entire season.

With a new coach and a new rotation to implement, the Liberty got off to a rocky start to the 2022 season, going 1-7 over the first few weeks of action. Sabrina

Ionescu was uncharacteristically inconsistent during this same stretch. She had 25 points, 4 rebounds, and 6 assists in the opener, but just 2 points in the second game. She then had 31 points, 3 rebounds, 7 assists, and even 4 steals in the Liberty's third game, but fell to just 2 points again two games later. It was a strange beginning to the season and very much gave New York the look of a team trying to figure out its identity.

During the next 10 games, the Liberty appeared to find some of that identity, and it started with Ionescu playing more freely and producing the way she is capable of. In the 10 games following the 1-7 start, Ionescu averaged 19.8 points, 7.6 rebounds, and 7.2 assists, shooting 44.6% from the field and 37.3% from three-point range. She also had a monster triple-double of 27 points, 13 rebounds, and 12 assists, albeit in a narrow loss to Chicago. It was unquestionably the best stretch of Ionescu's career to that point, and helped New York to a 7-3 streak that brought its record for the season to 8-10.

It also helped get Ionescu voted into the WNBA All-Star Game for the first time in her career. Before heading off to the July 10th All-Star Weekend, however, Ionescu had one more major performance up her sleeve. In the second-to-last game leading up to the break, the newly anointed All-Star racked up 31 points, 13 rebounds, and 10 assists in a win over the Las Vegas Aces, who were perhaps the most talented team in the league at the time. Notably, it was the first time in WNBA history that a player had scored 30 points as part of a triple-double; it also brought Ionescu up to three total triple-doubles for her career, tying the Chicago Sky's Candace Parker.

Ionescu's first trip to the WNBA's All-Star Weekend just a few days later proved to be something of an initiation. First and foremost, she seemed to be completely comfortable competing with some of the league's best talents in the annual showcase. Ionescu won the Saturday Skills Competition and, in the All-Star Game, she hit 4 three-pointers and finished with

19 points, 6 rebounds, and 6 assists to help secure a win for her team (named "Team Wilson" for its captain, A'ja Wilson).

Beyond the basketball, meanwhile, Ionescu was welcomed into the sisterhood of elite WNBA talents, so to speak, by none other than Candace Parker. The two had interacted on many prior occasions and had established a bond during the previous summer when Parker had told Ionescu not to play hurt while the two were competing at Barclays Center.

At the All-Star Game, Ionescu reflected that this had been a memorable moment for her—a time when she was supported on a very human level by a rival competitor. Now, however, they were peers. "It's amazing to watch," Parker said of Ionescu's comeback and All-Star selection.[xvi] "I'm all about bounce back, I'm all about getting back up and she's done that."

Returning to action after All-Star Weekend, the Liberty lost two in a row to the Aces, despite a 27-

point effort from Ionescu in the first game back. From there, however, New York went on a 7-5 run to close out the season, with Ionescu often flashing dominant form.

The All-Star guard sniffed another triple-double against the defending WNBA Champion Chicago Sky on July 23rd, finishing with 17 points, 8 rebounds, and 9 assists. She notched a career-high 16 assists in a terrific performance against Phoenix on July 31st. Almost immediately thereafter, she had a scorching run of four games during which she averaged 25.8 points.

The Liberty finished the regular season with a 16-20 record. It was by no means a major triumph, but still quite respectable, especially given the awful start to the season. As the team readied itself for a first-round playoff bout with the Chicago Sky, an article at the *New York Times* declared that we were finally all seeing "the Sabrina Ionescu we'd been waiting for."[xvii]

The same article said of Ionescu, "She has improved in almost every category, playing more minutes, shooting at a higher percentage, and increasing her rebounding, assists, and steals numbers while reducing her turnovers." The piece also noted that Ionescu's more prominent role in the New York offense had coincided with more team success.

Indeed, somewhere between the lead-up to the All-Star Game and the end of the season, something seemed to have clicked—college-quality Sabrina Ionescu was finally running the show for the Liberty.

In 2022, the WNBA playoff format shifted so that the first round was comprised of a three-game series. The Liberty thus got a few shots at the defending champs, albeit as a substantial underdog. In Game 1 at Chicago, New York shocked the entire WNBA, pulling off an upset win behind 22 points, 7 rebounds, and 6 assists from Sabrina Ionescu.

In the next two games, however, the Sky would assert themselves and display their dominance. Ionescu struggled in Game 2 as Chicago won big, and while she rebounded somewhat in the decisive third game, the Sky came out on top.

It was another first-round loss for Ionescu and the Liberty. As had happened throughout Ionescu's college career, however, her team seemed to be getting closer to greater accomplishments. In her freshman year in college, Oregon had been clobbered in the Elite 8 by UConn. Then, in the next season, they lost in the same round but were decidedly more competitive against a vaunted Notre Dame team. Similarly, in the 2021 WNBA Playoffs, the Liberty had been swept aside in a single playoff game (though Ionescu did have a desperate heave to try to win it in the closing seconds). Now, in 2022, New York actually won a playoff game, pushing just a little closer to advancing before being eliminated again.

One Step Closer to Championship Glory

Following another sub-.500 season and a second straight exit in the first round of the playoffs, the Liberty front office executed a massive overhaul leading up to the 2023 season. This began with a three-team mega-trade that saw the 6th pick in the 2023 Draft and Natasha Howard, in addition to other assets, sent away from New York. In return, the Liberty brought back 2021 MVP Jonquel Jones from the Connecticut Sun and Kayla Thornton from the Dallas Wings.

Next, New York signed 2018 MVP and two-time WNBA Champion Breanna Stewart, whose contract with the Seattle Storm had run its course. The Liberty also grabbed veteran All-Star and 2021 WNBA Champion Courtney Vandersloot away from the Chicago Sun and then set about taking care of their own by extending Sabrina Ionescu's contract to last through 2025 at least.

"We couldn't be more excited to announce Sabrina's multi-year extension," New York General Manager Jonathan Kolb said in a statement reported by ESPN.[xviii] "Her career is already off to a historic start and her will to win is truly unparalleled. Sab has quickly become synonymous with the Liberty franchise, and we look forward to her continued success in New York for many years to come."

Offering her own thoughts, Ionescu added, "I'm thankful and honored to be able to represent the New York Liberty for the next couple years ... Joe and Clara Wu Tsai, Jonathan Kolb, and the entire Liberty organization has been nothing short of amazing over my time here, and I'm thrilled to work towards bringing a championship back to New York City." She also expressed gratitude that the franchise had stuck with her through her first two seasons as she dealt with injuries, giving her the time to evolve into the star she has become at the pro level.

With multiple stars newly aboard and Sabrina Ionescu well taken care of, the Liberty approached the 2023 season with a fearsome new look. Breanna Stewart, Courtney Vandersloot, Betnijah Laney, Jonquel Jones, and Ionescu comprised as tough a starting lineup as there was in the WNBA, and Marine Johannes, Kayla Thornton, and Stefanie Dolson made for a strong bench core. Along with the equally super-powered Las Vegas Aces, the Liberty at last looked to be favorites for a WNBA title run.

New York stumbled a bit at the outset of the season with a lackluster loss to the Washington Mystics. Following a slow start, though, the Liberty blitzed their way through the first half of the season, going 14-4 up to the All-Star Break. This would be a very strong record for any team under any circumstances, but for the Liberty, to achieve it while fitting so many new players together on the fly was an impressive achievement.

These adjustments were perhaps particularly jarring for Sabrina Ionescu. Having been somewhat overburdened as New York's do-it-all superstar during the previous two seasons, she now found herself on a roster with a premium scorer and rebounder in Breanna "Stewie" Stewart and a legendary ball distributor in Courtney Vandersloot. This is not to say the scoring, rebounding, or assist loads were taken off Ionescu's shoulders. But, on this roster, her job changed. Now, rather than doing everything all the time, she could tap into her versatile nature and do what was needed on any given night. With this approach, Ionescu became less of a night-to-night triple-double threat but still mixed in towering performances.

Ionescu had 16 rebounds through New York's first two games, proving that she would still attack the boards despite having Stewie aboard to dominate in the paint. She scored a career-high 37 points in a game at Atlanta on June 9, 2023, hitting 8 of 13 three-point attempts in the effort. Just a few games later, Ionescu tallied 31 points on 7-for-12 three-point shooting against Washington. And, in early July, she had nine and then eight assists in back-to-back games, demonstrating that, despite Vandersloot's status as a passing maestro, Ionescu was still a lead guard.

The Liberty's final game before the All-Star Break doubled as the final regular season Commissioner's Cup game competition. New York faced off against Indiana, and Ionescu finished with 34 points, 6 rebounds, and 5 assists to lead the winning effort and assure the Liberty a place in the Cup Final.

Ionescu was voted into All-Star Weekend once again, and while she participated in the game for the second year in a row, the real highlight for her was the Three-Point Contest on Saturday. There, Ionescu not only won but also broke Stephen Curry's record for most points scored in such a competition in the WNBA or NBA! She finished with an astounding 37 points, thanks in large part to the fact that she made 25 of her final 27 shots. It was a scorching performance that drove home the point that Ionescu was subtly morphing into an elite outside shooting threat.

As they had done at the beginning of the season, the Liberty stumbled back into action after the break, losing by 10 to the Dallas Wings. After that, however, they went on another tear, rattling off emphatic wins one after the other. New York ultimately went 18-4 in games following All-Star Weekend, breaking the 100-point mark three times along the way. They also triumphed in the Commissioner's Cup Final on August 15th to capture the biggest trophy in franchise history.

Playing the Aces at Michelob Ultra Arena in Las Vegas, the Liberty triumphed 82-63, with Ionescu contributing 12 points, 8 rebounds, and 2 assists. Some took the win as a telling sign of things to come. Wrote Ryan Young for Yahoo Sports, "While it feels like this matchup could very well be a preview for the WNBA

Finals, the Liberty very clearly have the upper hand in the series right now. If the Aces are going to defend their title from last season, they'll have to find a way to get past New York."[xix]

Both before and after the Commissioner's Cup, Sabrina Ionescu's second half of the 2023 season marked one of the most consistent stretches of her career. She got back to her triple-double ways in a win over Seattle, posting 12 points, 12 rebounds, and 12 assists in 31 minutes. She reached 31 points on two separate occasions, first in a close loss to Minnesota and then in a blowout win over the Aces. Indeed, she scored in double digits in all but one of her games after All-Star Weekend. Overall, Ionescu averaged 17.6 points, 5.4 rebounds, 5.6 assists, and 1.1 steals over the course of the season's second half, shooting 44.4% from the field and 44.8% from three.

It appeared that the *New York Times* writer who had declared roughly a year ago that the Sabrina Ionescu we'd been waiting to see had finally shown up may have been a little early in that statement. Undoubtedly, *this* was the superstar version of Ionescu that most closely resembled her otherworldly college form.

On the back of Ionescu's efforts along with consistently stellar play from the likes of Stewie and Jones, the Liberty finished the regular season with a 32-8 record and the top spot in the Eastern Conference Playoffs. They entered a first-round, best-of-three-game series against the Washington Mystics and won 2-0 with relative ease. Ionescu hit 7 of 13 three-pointers for 29 points in Game 1. Her scoring effort was quieter in Game 2, but still managed to contribute 9 rebounds to do her part.

The Liberty next faced off with the Connecticut Sun in the Eastern Conference Finals in a best-of-five-game series. They stumbled in Game 1, losing by 15 at home as Stewie and Ionescu both struggled mightily from the field. New York bounced back quickly, however, sweeping the next three games to win the series and advance to the WNBA Finals. Sabrina Ionescu was not at her overpowering best, but still had a reasonably productive series.

The Finals produced the matchup that many had seen coming since before the 2023 season started—Liberty versus Aces in a best-of-five series. Throughout the season, the Liberty had appeared to have the upper hand in the matchup. As the Yahoo Sports recap of the Commissioner's Cup Final had predicted, the Aces would indeed have to find a way through New York if they were to defend their WNBA title.

Unfortunately for the Liberty faithful, however, this is just what ended up happening. Las Vegas seemed to find a new gear in the Finals, winning the first two games at home by a combined 45 points. The Liberty clawed their way back to win Game 3 in New York, but the Aces were, by that point, without star guard Chelsea Gray, who had suffered a series-ending injury.

And in Game 4, New York fell just short of extending the series. The Aces triumphed 70-69 to win the series 3-1 and capture a second consecutive WNBA Championship.

Throughout the series, Las Vegas had largely held the New York stars in check. Accordingly, Sabrina Ionescu's production had been limited. That said, she had displayed a tremendously poised floor game against a juggernaut opponent. For the series, she finished with 22 assists and just 5 turnovers.

Despite its bitter end, the 2023 season had been Ionescu's finest yet. She finished with averages of 17 points, 5.6 rebounds, and 5.4 rebounds per game, shooting 42.3% from the field and an astounding 44.8% from three-point range. She was voted to the All-WNBA second team for the second season in a row and collected a second All-Star appearance as well.

Most important, however, was that Ionescu had gotten one step closer to an elusive championship effort, too. Ionescu had ended her college career having knocked on the door of a national championship before being cruelly denied her final shot by the COVID-19 outbreak. She has now knocked similarly on the door of the WNBA title. But this time around, she may just get a few more chances to go all the way.

Chapter 5: International Career

Lots of good WNBA players spend their offseasons overseas playing for club teams in leagues around the world. This effectively serves two purposes. The first is that it provides them with high-level competition that can keep them sharp during what is ultimately a long annual off period for the WNBA. The second is that it gives them more opportunities to earn additional income to supplement their WNBA contracts, which are not typically as lucrative as those in many other professional sports and, sadly, not on par with contracts in the NBA.

Thus, many of the best players in the league take advantage of overseas opportunities to serve these purposes. Sabrina Ionescu, however, has yet to make a foray into a foreign league. There were indications that she may have considered doing so at the tail end of her rehab before the 2021 season, but she ultimately elected to stay in the United States.

Ionescu is still only 25 years old at the time of this writing. She is in an early stage of her career, and will have plenty more opportunities to play for a club overseas if she desires to do so. For the time being, however, she does not have this experience on her resume. She does, however, have the *other* kind of international experience that many of the top WNBA players can boast: She has enjoyed several different stints playing with USA Basketball at different levels of competition.

The first such stint occurred when Ionescu was still just a kid. In 2013, she got a chance to play in the FIBA Americas U-16 Championships in Cancun, Mexico. Still only 15 years old at the time, she was among the youngest members of the U.S. team, which was led by Asia Durr and Katie Lou Samuelson—both a class ahead of Ionescu. Nevertheless, Ionescu played in all five games for the U.S., averaging 3.4 points, 3.8 rebounds, and 2 assists (good for fifth-best in the tournament field) in 17.6 minutes per game. It was invaluable experience for the emerging prospect, and, as a bonus, Team USA won all five of its games, ultimately defeating Canada 82-48 for a gold medal.

The following summer, a 16-year-old Sabrina Ionescu got another opportunity to suit up for a junior national team. Once again, Asia Durr and Katie Lou Samuelson would be leading the way, and once again, Ionescu would be among the youngest girls competing.

This time around, however, the tournament was held in the Czech Republic with a FIBA U-17 World Cup medal on the line. The U.S. team breezed through group play with a 3-0 record and had a relatively easy time with the knock-outs as well. Then, the Americans scraped by a formidable Spanish team in the gold medal round to win the tournament's top prize. Ionescu had again played a relatively limited role in terms of total production, but she had led the team in assists on two occasions—first with five against China in group play, and again with five more in a Round of 16 matchup with Mexico.

Ionescu's next two forays into Team USA competition were a little more unorthodox. This is because she and some of her friends from the team at Oregon happened to get in on 3x3 basketball almost as soon as it was legitimized in international competition.

It started in April of 2018 when Ionescu traveled with Ducks teammates Erin Boley, Otiona Gildon, and Ruthy Hebard to the Olympic Training Center in Colorado Springs to participate in USA Basketball's national 3x3 tournament. With the exception of Boley, the group had virtually no experience with official 3x3 basketball, let alone playing together in such an event. In the end, though, their team (the "Oregon Ducks," of course!) went 8-0 in the competition, defeating team Bye Felicia in the final.

Ionescu earned MVP honors, but said afterward, "I'm just happy we won, to be honest. The individual award doesn't mean as much as winning the gold with this squad."[xx]

The experience that Ionescu and Hebard gained together would prove to mean quite a lot as well because those two would be back for the 2019 Pan-American Games' 3x3 competition in Lima, Peru in 2019. They joined up with UConn players Olivia Nelson-Ododa and Christyn Williams to comprise the U.S. team and promptly rolled to a 5-0 record in group play. The Americans then beat Brazil 21-5 in the semifinals behind 9 points from Ionescu, and topped Argentina in a tight, 21-17 final. Ionescu and Hebard tied for the lead with 7 points each in this championship bout as Team USA captured the gold medal once again.

The 3x3 tournament at the Lima Pan-American Games represented Ionescu's final experience with USA Basketball before her professional career began. Altogether, counting her time with junior national teams and in 3x3 tournaments, she had already collected four gold medals. In 2022, however, Sabrina finally got an opportunity to play with the senior national team.

Fresh off her first All-Star season in the WNBA, she made it onto a roster full of established, veteran stars such as Breanna Stewart, A'ja Wilson, Kelsey Plum, and Alyssa Thomas. That group led Team USA to Sydney, Australia, for the FIBA World Cup in late September following the WNBA season. Together, they dominated the field, rolling to a 5-0 record in group play, cruising to the final, and then dispatching China to win the gold.

With so many accomplished superstars on the roster, Ionescu played a reserve role in this first senior national team experience. In 12.8 minutes per game across 7 appearances, though, she still managed to average 3 points, 2.1 rebounds, and an impressive 2 assists per game.

As of this writing, Sabrina Ionescu's tally across all levels of Team USA competition is five gold medals. It is widely believed that she will add to that number before all is said and done. Notably, USA Basketball has already held training camps in preparation for the Summer Olympics in Paris in 2024. Ionescu is among the headliners participating at this early stage, along with Kelsey Plum, Brittney Griner, and invaluable veteran Diana Taurasi, whom many consider to be the best women's basketball player in history. Sabrina and her powerhouse USA teammates will undoubtedly be looking to add to their pile of gold in Paris next summer.

Chapter 6: Personal Life

Most of what we know about Sabrina Ionescu's personal life tends to concern her family and close friends. It has been clear throughout the years, for instance, that Sabrina has remained close with her parents and brothers—with, of course, a special bond existing between the basketball star and her twin brother, Eddy. That the family has managed to stay close despite Sabrina's meteoric rise to basketball stardom and busy schedule is a testament to the depth of their connections.

Sabrina is also known to be particularly good friends with her former Oregon and USA 3x3 teammate, Ruthy Hebard. While other talented players came and went during their four years at Oregon, it was these two who led the turnaround of the program. To hear those around the Oregon team tell it, they did so just as much on the strength of their friendship as the complementary nature of their games.

Said Ducks coach Kelly Graves as Oregon prepared to see Ionescu and Hebard off on their senior night, "They were just the perfect marriage for each other. It's crazy that it worked out this way."[xxi] He added, "There's a real love for each other that I've seen develop since the time they were freshmen."

When talking of Sabrina Ionescu's friends and family, it is also necessary at this point to mention the Bryants. While Sabrina experienced unexpected tragedy upon the shocking passing of Kobe Bryant and his daughter Gigi, the bond she has since formed with the Bryant family has been nothing short of remarkable. She is known to have stayed in close contact with Vanessa Bryant, Kobe's wife, as well as surviving daughters Natalia, Bianka, and Capri. Sabrina has spent time at the Bryants' home and has met with them after some of her own professional games.

On the romantic front, very little was ever made public about Sabrina until early in 2023 when she announced that she had become engaged to boyfriend Hroniss Grasu. A fellow Californian athlete of Romanian descent, Grasu played football at the University of Oregon, though the two were not in Eugene at the same time. Grasu was drafted to the NFL just before Ionescu started her spectacular career with the Ducks. As of now, he plays as a backup center for the Las Vegas Raiders.

As of September, Ionescu and Grasu were said to be "a couple months away" from tying the knot.[xxii] That said, Ionescu also told the *New York Post* that she hadn't done any planning yet on the grounds that both are very busy. "The wedding will happen in the offseason," she clarified, adding that she was excited. "That's obviously gonna be one of the greatest days of my life." (Ever the competitor, she noted that she hoped a championship would soon mark one of those days as well.)

"It's a great love story," she has said of her engagement. "A little Oregon Ducks love story."

Chapter 7: Impact and Legacy

Sabrina Ionescu's impact on basketball is both enormous and, as of yet, immeasurable. This is largely because Sabrina is only 25 years old at the time of this writing. She is not merely young or in the middle of her career. Rather, she may well still be at the very *beginning* of it. Provided that she enjoys good health, Ionescu could easily play for another decade or more. And when one recalls that most of her first season and a good portion of her second were compromised due to injury, it is not unreasonable to look at her as a player who is just getting started. The 2024 season will be only her third full, healthy season in the WNBA.

Despite her youth and status as a still-emerging star, however, it is also fair to say that Ionescu has already impacted the game and firmly established herself as a force to be reckoned with. In her time as an NCAA athlete, she collected a dizzying array of records and awards, all but redefining what was possible for a college basketball player. She rewrote the Oregon and Pac-12 record books, set a new mark for triple-doubles among men *or* women at the college level, and effectively put the Ducks' women's basketball program on the map.

Furthermore, Sabrina did all this as a child of immigrants, took an unorthodox path, as she eschewed paid trainers for the playground and shrugged off major college programs to chart her own way. Without a doubt, Ionescu showed countless kids and young players around the world that it was possible to achieve great success without following in tried-and-true, traditional footsteps. She was as inspiring a player as college sports have seen in this century, showing remarkable grit and determination along with a will to take whatever team she plays for to the pinnacles of success.

At the WNBA level, perhaps Ionescu's greatest impact so far has been in helping to spark a triple-double revolution that is likely just getting started. She has clearly demonstrated that a triple-double phenom could truly rise in the college ranks and WNBA with an alacrity that rivaled and at times even eclipsed her male counterparts in the NBA.

This is not to merely say that Ionescu has inspired interest in specific statistical achievements; the triple-double in modern basketball is not only about the numbers. Rather, it is about the style of play required to approach those kinds of numbers. Sabrina Ionescu is a gifted, natural scorer who could easily have devoted her career to amassing as many points as she could in each game and at every level.

Indeed, in recent seasons, she has shown that she is only improving as a shooter, meaning that she may get even better at simply putting the ball in the basket as her career progresses. Instead of focusing only on scoring, however, Ionescu has prioritized smart basketball and team play above all. In the simplest terms, she seeks to make the play that is needed, whether that means she needs to score, pass, rebound, or try for a steal. In this way, Ionescu is leading a wave of complete basketball, showcasing the idea that being *good* at everything can make you a *great* player. If this lesson takes hold with young fans and emerging players, Ionescu will have left a remarkable legacy on the court.

It can also be said that Sabrina Ionescu's impact and legacy away from the court are incomplete as well. Already in her young career, she has shown to have natural influence as well as a keen interest in business and philanthropic efforts. It stands to reason that, as time goes on and her success continues to mount, Ionescu will find more ways to impact the people and communities around her. While we undoubtedly have much to look forward to on this front, though, there is also another interesting part of her legacy that is already taking shape.

For Ionescu, a portion of that legacy starts with the University of Oregon, which quite clearly still has her heart. In 2022, the Liberty star rejoined her alma mater as a part-time Director of Athletic Culture. In this capacity, Sabrina is aiming to help develop student-athletes in Eugene according to her former college coach's "five pillars of Oregon women's basketball," which are passion, integrity, unity, thankfulness, and servanthood.

Referring to the university as the place where she joined her second family, Ionescu said of her intentions with the role, "Part of my heart remains in Eugene, and I look forward to cultivating the same family atmosphere for future Ducks in the Oregon women's basketball program."[xxiii]

The University of Oregon also served as the first location for a youth basketball camp connected to the SI20 Foundation, which itself represents arguably Ionescu's most ambitious effort to give back to date. In

Eugene in 2022, Ionescu organized a camp for 250 kids from fourth to eighth grade that was split across two sessions. The kids got an opportunity to learn about basketball and life from Ionescu and some of her own mentors.

An SI.com article on this inaugural camp for the SI20 Foundation made the observation that Ionescu did not have this kind of opportunity to soak up pro-caliber instruction when she was growing up. In fact, she was not even able to play for her middle school initially. This may explain why the WNBA star appears to be so moved and humbled to give back the way she does.

"It's something you can't always put into words," she said about hosting the camp.[xxiv] "Maybe when I'm done playing, I'll be able to look back and think about how cool that really is. But even now, it's kind of humbling and honoring to be able to do that coming from how far that I've come through my basketball career, and now being able to give back and hopefully inspire young kids..." She added that she did not take the opportunity for granted.

This first kids' camp was special to Ionescu because she put it together in Eugene. Ultimately, however, the intention behind the SI20 Foundation is to provide more widespread opportunities to engage through sports and communities across the country. An extensive *Forbes* profile on Ionescu's assorted business interests described the foundation's purpose as being to "equip youth from all backgrounds and skill levels with equitable access to sports to create genuine connections and build stronger communities for life."[xxv] It will be fascinating to see what Ionescu does with a foundation of this nature in the years to come.

That same *Forbes* profile made it clear that, while Ionescu is deeply focused on giving back through the SI20 foundation, she has also become a formidable businesswoman. With some guidance from NBA greats Kevin Durant and Steph Curry, Ionescu has gotten involved with a number of different businesses. She and her representatives have forged relationships with the likes of Body Armor, State Farm, Nike, and Xbox. She is an ambassador for Durant's Boardroom media company and a partner with Thirty Five Ventures (aka 35V), Durant's venture capital outfit. Plus, she has invested with companies such as Nex and Buzzer Media. Collectively, these business interests and the savvy way in which Ionescu appears to navigate them helped her land a place among *Forbes's* "30 Under 30" list for 2023.

It is ultimately her Nike partnership, though, that may represent Sabrina Ionescu's most profound impact away from the court. While lots of athletes have endorsement deals in place to represent certain apparel manufacturers, Ionescu has gone above and beyond to take advantage of the company's resources and have a say in her partnership.

In the aforementioned *Forbes* profile, Nike senior footwear designer Benjamin Nethongkome praised the Liberty star for making requests and demonstrating awareness more like that of a "more seasoned athlete."

This high praise concerned the collaborative effort to design Ionescu's first signature shoe with Nike. And it is that shoe that has tremendously expanded her impact on the game. This is because the shoe is made for both women *and* men.

"My main goal was wanting a unisex shoe to give opportunity for girls, boys, anyone to wear the shoe. I was excited to continue to break down barriers and wanted to do that with them, who also believe in that as well," Ionescu told *Forbes*.

The significance of this is twofold. First, it gives girls and women everywhere a beautifully designed and well-marketed shoe associated with an extremely popular women's player. Second, it invites boys and men to participate in the phenomenon of Sabrina

Ionescu, and by extension, take a greater interest in women's sports. Not for nothing, a handful of prominent professionals have already gotten on board. Most won't be surprised to learn that Ionescu teammates Jonquel Jones and Courtney Vandersloot have already been spotted wearing Sabrina 1 shoes in competition. Some will be more surprised, however, to find out that a handful of prominent NBA players have gotten on board as well. Cam Payne, Jordan Clarkson, and Jrue Holiday are among the NBA pros who have worn Sabrina 1s in games.

When you consider all of these individual accomplishments, her budding impact and influence, and the pieces of legacy already falling into place together, you begin to see Sabrina Ionescu's career for what it can really be in its entirety. Through her style of play and success, her determination to support her college program, her advocacy for kids' basketball and communities, and her inclusive, unisex apparel,

Ionescu seems to exist for the purpose of *growing basketball*.

Of course, her gaudy stats, relentless drive to win, and rising number of triple-doubles alone would bring more eyes to women's basketball. However, she is not content with just that. Sabrina Ionescu wants the *action*, and so far, she's spent much of her career off the court providing opportunities for others to engage and fall in love with the sport that has given her so much.

Final Word/About the Author

I was born and raised in Norwalk, Connecticut. Growing up, I could often be found spending many nights watching basketball, soccer, and football matches with my father in the family living room. I love sports and everything that sports can embody. I believe that sports are one of the most genuine forms of competition, heart, and determination. I write my works to learn more about influential athletes in the hopes that from my writing, you the reader can walk away inspired to put in an equal if not greater amount of hard work and perseverance to pursue your goals. If you enjoyed *Sabrina Ionescu: The Inspiring Story of One of Basketball's Star Guards*, please leave a review! Also, you can read more of my works on *David Ortiz, Aroldis Chapman, Trea Turner, Freddie Freeman, Marcus Stroman, Kris Bryant, Corey Seager, Jose Bautista, Salvador Perez, Cody Bellinger, Alex Bregman, Francisco Lindor, Shohei Ohtani, Ronald Acuna Jr., Javier Baez, Jose Altuve, Christian*

Yelich, Max Scherzer, Mookie Betts, Pete Alonso, Clayton Kershaw, Mike Trout, Bryce Harper, Jackie Robinson, Justin Verlander, Derek Jeter, Ichiro Suzuki, Ken Griffey Jr., Babe Ruth, Mariano Rivera, Xander Bogaerts, Yuli Gurriel, Buster Posey, Edwin Diaz, Juan Soto, Aaron Judge, Novak Djokovic, Roger Federer, Andy Roddick, Rafael Nadal, Serena Williams, Naomi Osaka, Caroline Wozniacki, Coco Gauff, Baker Mayfield, Jalen Hurts, Saquon Barkley, Kirk Cousins, DK Metcalf, Christian McCaffrey, Nick Chubb, George Kittle, Matt Ryan, Travis Kelce, Matthew Stafford, Alvin Kamara, Eli Manning, Khalil Mack, Davante Adams, Terry Bradshaw, Jimmy Garoppolo, Philip Rivers, Tua Tagovailoa, Von Miller, Aaron Donald, Joey Bosa, Kyler Murray, Josh Allen, Mike Evans, Joe Burrow, Carson Wentz Adam Thielen, Stefon Diggs, Lamar Jackson, Dak Prescott, Patrick Mahomes, Odell Beckham Jr., J.J. Watt, Colin Kaepernick, Aaron Rodgers, Tom Brady, Russell Wilson, Peyton Manning, Drew Brees, Calvin

Johnson, Brett Favre, Rob Gronkowski, Andrew Luck, Richard Sherman, Bill Belichick, Candace Parker, Maya Moore, Kelsey Plum, Elena Delle Donne, Skylar Diggins-Smith, A'ja Wilson, Lisa Leslie, Sue Bird, Diana Taurasi, Julius Erving, Shai Gilgeous-Alexander, Zach LaVine, Karl-Anthony Towns, Clyde Drexler, John Havlicek, Oscar Robertson, Ja Morant, Gary Payton, Khris Middleton, Michael Porter Jr., Julius Randle, Jrue Holiday, Domantas Sabonis, Mike Conley Jr., Jerry West, Dikembe Mutombo, Fred VanVleet, Jamal Murray, Zion Williamson, Brandon Ingram, Jaylen Brown, Charles Barkley, Trae Young, Andre Drummond, JJ Redick, DeMarcus Cousins, Wilt Chamberlain, Bradley Beal, Rudy Gobert, Aaron Gordon, Kristaps Porzingis, Nikola Vucevic, Andre Iguodala, Devin Booker, John Stockton, Jeremy Lin, Chris Paul, Pascal Siakam, Jayson Tatum, Gordon Hayward, Nikola Jokic, Bill Russell, Victor Oladipo, Luka Doncic, Ben Simmons, Shaquille O'Neal, Joel Embiid, Donovan Mitchell, Damian Lillard, Giannis

Antetokounmpo, Chris Bosh, Kemba Walker, Isaiah Thomas, DeMar DeRozan, Amar'e Stoudemire, Al Horford, Yao Ming, Marc Gasol, Draymond Green, Kawhi Leonard, Dwyane Wade, Ray Allen, Pau Gasol, Dirk Nowitzki, Jimmy Butler, Paul Pierce, Manu Ginobili, Pete Maravich, Larry Bird, Kyle Lowry, Jason Kidd, David Robinson, LaMarcus Aldridge, Derrick Rose, Paul George, Kevin Garnett, Michael Jordan, LeBron James, Kyrie Irving, Klay Thompson, Stephen Curry, Kevin Durant, Russell Westbrook, Chris Paul, Blake Griffin, Kobe Bryant, Anthony Davis, Joakim Noah, Scottie Pippen, Carmelo Anthony, Kevin Love, Grant Hill, Tracy McGrady, Vince Carter, Patrick Ewing, Karl Malone, Tony Parker, Allen Iverson, Hakeem Olajuwon, Reggie Miller, Michael Carter-Williams, James Harden, John Wall, Tim Duncan, Steve Nash, Toni Kroos, Neymar, Paul Pogba, Harry Kane, Robert Lewandowski, Jack Grealish, Mohamed Salah, Gareth Bale, Gregg Popovich, Pat Riley, John Wooden, Steve Kerr, Brad

Stevens, Red Auerbach, Doc Rivers, Erik Spoelstra, Mike D'Antoni and Phil Jackson in the Kindle Store. If you love basketball, check out my website at claytongeoffreys.com to join my exclusive list where I let you know about my latest books and give you lots of goodies.

Like what you read? Please leave a review!

I write because I love sharing the stories of influential athletes like Sabrina Ionescu with fantastic readers like you. My readers inspire me to write more so please do not hesitate to let me know what you thought by leaving a review! If you love books on life, basketball, or productivity, check out my website at claytongeoffreys.com to join my exclusive list where I let you know about my latest books. Aside from being the first to hear about my latest releases, you can also download a free copy of *33 Life Lessons: Success Principles, Career Advice & Habits of Successful People*. See you there!

Clayton

References

[i] "Inside The WNBA's Triple-Double Explosion". *ESPN.com. 17 May* 2023. Web.
[ii] Merrill, Elizabeth. "Will Sabrina Ionescu's Basketball Obsession Play In Oregon's Favor?". *ESPN.co.uk.* 22 March 2019. Web.
[iii] Wallace, Ava. "Her Middle School Said To Play With Dolls. She Set An NCAA Triple-Double Record Instead". *WashingtonPost.com.* 4 February 2019. Web.
[iv] Villa, Walter. "Sabrina Ionescu Makes Big Impression". *SECSports.com.* 11 July 2013. Web.
[v] Nemec, Andrew. "Sabrina Ionescu, McDonald's All-American MVP, Commits To Oregon Ducks". *OregonLive.com.* 19 June 2016. Web.
[vi] Richmond, Ron. "Sabrina Ionescu Sets NCAA Mark For Triple-Doubles In Oregon's Win Over Washington". *Spokesman*.com. 31 December 2017. Web.
[vii] Associated Press. "Oregon's Ionescu Gets 13th Triple-Double, Sets NCAA Record". *APNews.com.* 20 December 2018. Web.
[viii] Ionescu, Sabrina. "A Letter To Ducks Nation". *ThePlayersTribune.com.* 7 April 2019. Web.
[ix] Hays, Graham. "Sabrina Ionescu's Career Night Leads Oregon Past Stanford". *ESPN.com.* 16 January 2020. Web.
[x] Ligons, Jordan. "The Ringer's 2020 WNBA Mock Draft". *TheRinger.com.* 15 April 2020. Web.
[xi] D'Arcangelo, Lyndsey. "The Athletic's 2020 WNBA Mock Draft: How Will It Unfold After No.1?". *TheAthletic.com.* 15 April 2020. Web.
[xii] Megdal, Howard. "Liberty Select Sabrina Ionescu No.1 In W.N.B.A. Draft". *NYTimes.com.* 17 April 2020. Web.
[xiii] Stein, Marc. "Sabrina Ionescu Opens Up About Kobe Bryant And Rookie Year Woes". *NYTimes.com.* 23 September 2020. Web.
[xiv] Cash, Meredith. "WNBA Star Sabrina Ionescu Wants A Second Rookie Year, But The WNBA Won't Budge". *Insider.com.* 30 April 2021. Web.
[xv] Skopil, Erik. "Sabrina Ionescu Missing Time With Injury To Same Ankle". *247Sports.com.* 14 June 2021. Web.
[xvi] McCord, AJ. "Sabrina Ionescu Shines At Her 1st WNBA All-Star Weekend". *OregonLive.com.* 10 July 2022. Web.
[xvii] Mather, Victor. "This Is The Sabrina Ionescu We Were Waiting For". *NYTimes.com.* 17 August 2022. Web.
[xviii] Philippou, Alexa. "Liberty Sign Sabrina Ionescu To Extension Through 2025". *ESPN.com.* 15 May 2023. Web.

[xix] Young, Ryan. "Commissioner's Cup: Sabrina Ionescu, Jonquel Jones And Liberty Shut Down Aces To Win Title". *Sports.Yahoo.com*. 15 August 2023. Web.

[xx] Skopil, Erik. "Ducks sweep competition, win National 3-on-3 Championship". *247sports.com*. 22 April 2018. Web.

[xxi] Skopil, Erik. "Sabrina Ionescu And Ruthy Hebard Will Be Linked Together Forever". *247Sports.com*. 29 February 2020. Web.

[xxii] Lemoncelli, Jenna. "Sabrina Ionescu's Getting Married Soon And Hasn't Planned A Single Thing". *NYPost.com*. 15 September 2023. Web.

[xxiii] Ayala, Erica L. "Sabrina Ionescu Joins Oregon Ducks In Part-Time Role". *Forbes.com*. 11 November 2022. Web.

[xxiv] Reubenking, Dylan. "EXCLUSIVE: Sabrina Ionescu Giving Back To Eugene Community With First Youth Basketball Camp". *SI.com*. 16 March 2022. Web.

[xxv] LoRé, Michael. "Sabrina Ionescu Building Her Business Off The Court By Learning From The Best". *Forbes.com*. 12 September 2023. Web.

Made in the USA
Monee, IL
22 January 2025